TRUCK STOP

LACHLAN PHILPOTT

CURRENCY PRESS
SYDNEY

CURRENCY PLAYS

First published in 2012
by Currency Press Pty Ltd,
PO Box 2287, Strawberry Hills, NSW, 2012, Australia
enquiries@currency.com.au
www.currency.com.au
in association with
Q Theatre Company, Penrith NSW

This revised edition published 2014

Cataloguing-in-Publication data for this title is available from the National Library of Australia website: www.nla.gov.au.

Typeset by Stefania Cox for Currency Press.
Cover illustration and design by Lisa White.

Currency Press acknowledges the Traditional Owners of the Country on which we live and work. We pay our respects to all Aboriginal and Torres Strait Islander Elders, past and present.

Contents

Introduction
  Chris Mead   *v*

TRUCK STOP   1

For Katrina

INTRODUCTION

I realised something profound about playwrights when I had the privilege of being part of a forum with Lachlan Philpott at the National Institute of Dramatic Art (NIDA)—organised by their Head of Playwriting, Jane Bodie in 2011. It was something that perhaps I had always known but never seen so clearly as I did that evening in Sydney's Kensington: playwrights are angry. And it was Lachlan who made it plain—he spoke with force and vigour about the compulsion to write drama, an impulse fuelled by real anger about the world that confronts his characters.

In my experience it's often been the case that playwrights—curious, sensitive and thoughtful types, great observers with prodigious memories, wicked senses of humour and ethnographic ears—once they start to enter the worlds of their plays, or recall the conditions out of which a play of theirs has emerged, they often become tetchy, cranky or just plain angry. I don't know enough novelists, poets or screen-writers to make an observation about all writers, but in my neck of the creative woods playwrights create when their internal infernos burst into the maelstrom of competing voices that are their plays. I am not suggesting that playwriting is all uncontrolled rancour, but I do contend that anger is a powerful motivating factor for playwrights as they look back, around and forward, and then begin to write. That plays rely on conflict seems a reductive truism—theatre's great value is as a crucible for molten, chaotic humanity, humanity rendered into art by a playwright's principled fury.

And playwrights take nothing for granted—every commonplace convention, unchallenged principle, social nicety, unnoticed glance, misspoken utterance, all are grist for their mill, all present opportunities to cut to a character's tormented core. They do this to show us suffering and striving, anguish that reveals greater truths and ultimately gives audiences a meaningful experience. Of course playwrights have intellectual, journalistic and poetic impulses but there's something inexorable and undeniable about the visceral link between emotion, memory, passion, story and audience. If you ever have the pleasure of meeting Lachlan Philpott you will think I am the mad one—but dwelling just below his cheeky and charming carapace is a sharp-eyed witness, a belligerent decrier of injustice and a deep, sometimes pugilistic, thinker on discrimination, disenfranchisement and the politics of everyday living.

Truck Stop reveals Lachlan's interest in giving voice to those on the margins of the Australian city. The setting for *Truck Stop* is literally on the edge of Sydney's vast conurbations, a last stop before a sparsely populated interior of immense distances. His characters struggle to be heard in a society and culture that has little respect for what they have to say, or especially, for the way they say it. This is a play that creates a forum for their voices to emerge in all their contradictory impulses, rage and joy. Lachlan presents quotidian worlds of casual violence, sexism, racism and class division all the while crafting characters of real grace and dignity. He also upturns the all-too-familiar Australian notion of an endless relaxed, articulate and comfortable middle class. And that's a remarkable feature of the play—while the playwright may be fired up by inequality and deprivation, the play is not a bilious political tirade, or worthy tract of moral redemption, but a drama alive with ambiguity and complexity, itself an incitement to further discourse.

Coming to playwriting from actor training and high school teaching Lachlan has a particular gift for the distillation of real voices. The transmission of marginalised voices is a political act in his work—to speak difficult, sometimes unpalatable, truths about disadvantage, rebellion, aberrance and otherness—and this begs interesting questions about authenticity and authority. For quite some time towards the end of the twentieth century theatre-makers were perplexed by the question of who had the right to tell certain stories. Could men write believable women characters? Could the middle aged accurately put words in the mouths of the young? Could, or even should, other classes try to represent the working class? Or was that in itself an act of colonisation, theft or repression? Indeed can the rational possibly speak of recklessness or anarchy? These are questions further complicated by notions of a work's authenticity. If a play is penned by an ex-school teacher mightn't it inevitably obscure and misunderstand the argot of the young? And wouldn't that same play also potentially (however subtly) portray authority figures as venerable battlers, everyday heroes struggling to help their messed-up charges, young people the play actually patronised and condescended to?

Truck Stop places young women at its heart, overcoming such niggling doubts and problematics by presenting multiple points of view using varied vocal registers. The characters describe their own worlds with their own words and the narration tells the story of key character decisions, decisions that are often self-defeating. That Lachlan has listened very carefully to the polyphony around him is evident. There is a genuine grittiness and accuracy to this language, but also a richness and sophistication. These characters are poetic and inarticulate, chatty and powerfully silent, intimate, yet resist easy explanation. Lachlan writes roles actors want to play because of their intricacy, loquaciousness and inner fires. Such characterisation allows certain issues to be aired—the alienation of the young, dispossession, the failing public education project, desensitisation to basic humanity, the perceived boredom of the suburbs, family trauma, the widening gap between the rich and the poor, the manifold responsibilities of those in authority, the seduction and danger of alcohol and drugs, the thin line between sexual experimentation and exploitation—through the prism of the experiential.

One of the key metaphorical systems at work within the play is referred to directly at the opening and the closing of the play— protection. The play dramatises rich questions about whose job it is to protect the almost legal—shifting the locus from the more common 'why', to the more pragmatic 'how'. Young adults are smart and they know a great deal but most would agree they still need to be sheltered, or learn how to begin to best shield themselves. The play opens with a seemingly unprovoked playground fight and we watch as the three 'SKANKS' increasingly abandon the safe and the sensible, with all reasonable safeguards failing or wilfully being cast aside—and indeed we are even protected from the truck-stop incidents themselves until the final pages. Over the course of the play Sam, Kelly and Aisha oscillate in the twilight between childhood and adulthood, naïvety and invulnerability, fierceness and fragility. Sam and Kelly love hating their lives and Aisha watches her new friends spiral out of control, but what can, should or must she do? And this rich dramatic question is thrown

squarely at us—what would we do? What should we do? Young girls
are trafficked at truck stops, how could this happen in Australia? And
what if it's their choice? If we are morally or ethically challenged,
emotionally distraught or just simply appalled, this is a play that seems
to suggest that our response might need to move beyond the knee-jerk
disciplining of young women or politician's insistent and simplistic
calls for law and order solutions to a deeper systemic re-thinking of
schooling, socialisation and community services.

One final quality worth noting about this play is its form. One of
the most difficult aspects of storytelling is matching content with form;
that is, how best to let the actual construction of the story—plot and
characters and their articulation of their world—be informed by and
reflect the guts of the story itself? This is something that Lachlan works
very hard to get right. This is a play that, typically for Lachlan, takes
on questions about who tells stories and who controls the lives of the
young. As a result, the stories are narrated by the subjects themselves—
sometimes in unison and sometimes solo. That this is a modern play
is obvious (ordinary people, swearing, pop songs and so on), but this
is especially so in the way Lachlan uses both mimesis and diegesis to
let the character tell their own stories. Through suggestion, nuance
and fine detail, powerful denotation and precise connotation this story
poses questions about how truths are constructed, witnessed and felt.
Scenes are set, events are narrated and attitudes illustrated through the
characters' own words and their mutable subjectivities, subjectivities
literally under construction but also under attack, subject to endemic
violence, systems failure and psychic disintegration. As the characters'
public and private voices are shared with us, Lachlan frames a meta-
narrative about which stories are being told and to whom. Not all plays
look like this on the page and Lachlan uses character voices to do all
the work. He uses this access to language to increase our intimacy with
the characters and their worlds but also uses it to hold us at bay, just as
the language of officialdom diffuses, decentres and discombobulates.
Language is our friend but it also wounds, blinds and evades.

And ultimately that's what makes theatre so compelling: intimacy
and evasion, knowing and unknowing, the gut response and the urge
to analyse. Further, this hints at why anger is so important in the
genesis of theatre—the initiating impulse that connects the rational

and the furious, the diagnostic and the affecting, the social survey and the immersive, all synthesised in the controlled polyphony of drama. Playwrights write out of anger because something matters to them—and when it strikes a chord it clearly matters to many of us. *Truck Stop* uses theatre to put issues of real social importance on stage without bombast or pomposity. Lachlan achieves this by putting real characters in impossible and impossibly familiar situations. We watch and laugh and squirm as they variously confront the recognisable, the difficult and the appalling, making understandable but ultimately disastrous choices. The social and political conditions that make this possible have made the playwright angry, and we feel the power of this anger through the characters and the story. And perhaps as a result we begin to look at the world anew—and maybe even, as Brecht instructed us in *The Measures Taken*, to change the world. It needs it.

Chris Mead
May 2012

Chris Mead is Literary Director at Melbourne Theatre Company.

ACKNOWLEDGEMENTS:

Thanks to Dramaturg Francesca Smith and the artists who have contributed to the development of this play: Kristy Best, Elena Carapetis, Leah De Niese, Katrina Douglas, Laura Hopkinson, Kylie Hiscock, Chris Mead, Elizabeth Nabben, Eryn Jean Norvill, Jane Phegan, Shari Sebbens, Sabrin Teó, Jess Tovey and Janine Watson.

Thanks also to Crowded Fire Theatre San Francisco, Q Theatre, MKA Theatre, Cate Carey, Mark Denny and Drama Students from Springwood High School, Susanna Dowling, Kylie Druett, Sue MacDonald and Drama Students from Chifley Senior College Mt Druitt, Peter Moses and Alicia Talbot.

Truck Stop was first produced by the Q Theatre Company, Penrith, on Wednesday 23 May 2012, with the following cast:

SAM	Eryn Jean Norvill
KELLY	Jessica Tovey
AISHA	Kristy Best
JOSIE/ MICHELLE/ CHARMAINE/ INDHU/ BRUCE/ NURSE/ SEX WORKER / MISS/ TATUM/ ROBBO/NAT/ TRENT/ TORQUAN /NOAH/ ROWSE	Elena Carapetis

Director, Katrina Douglas
Set and Costume Designer, Michael Hankin
Sound Designer, Peter Kennard
Video Designer, Sean Bacon
Lighting Designer, Chris Page
Production Manager, Annette Rowlison
Stage Manager, Emma Taite

CHARACTERS:

Truck Stop can be played by four actors in the following combination:

SAM
KELLY
AISHA
JOSIE/ MICHELLE/ CHARMAINE/ INDHU/ BRUCE/ NURSE/ SEX WORKER/
MISS/ TATUM/ ROBBO/ NAT/ TRENT/ TORQUAN /NOAH/ ROWSE.

NOTE ON TEXT:

/	indicates point of interruption and/or overlap.
SAM/KELLY:	indicates lines to be said simultaneously, with assignment of lines to correspond to placement of character's name.
…	indicates unfinished sentence.
[ ]	bracketed words for actor's information, not delivery.

Since pop stars come in and out of vogue so fast, the Ke$ha lyrics used may need to be altered to fit the day of performance.

Projection: We see Sam and Kelly perform in a dance concert at age 10.

The girls, now 14, enter and sit at a roadside picnic table. The projection morphs to a busy highway, traffic coming at us.

We hear a CB radio, a vague conversation between two men, rich with static interference.

There is a sharp slapping sound like a whip.

Black.

AISHA: In the middle of the quad that day Kelly walks up to Sam and slaps her in the face. Slap like a cracking whip. Everyone hears it. Stops.

Sam shakes her head, turns away, turns back, runs at Kelly, pushes her to the ground, punches her in the face. Kelly snatches Sam's hair, twists it round her wrist, pulls her by the hair, looks her in the eye, spits in her face.

Kids circle them, phones held overhead.

Teacher pushes through the ring, rips Sam and Kelly apart.

Teacher yells, spits anger in their faces. Two sides he's saying. Two sides to every story.

Everyone says that.

> KELLY *returns and sits at the picnic table with a plastic water cup and drinks.*

Miss Rowse, the headmistress, stands in front of the whole school and raves on about protection. The school gates protect you from the outside, your parents and your friends protect you, look out for you. Her voice drops to almost a whisper as she says *but you still need to protect yourselves.*

> SAM *is beside* KELLY *but it is evident they are now in a different place.* KELLY *crushes the cup.*

The story about the Truck Stop has more than two sides.

Jessica Tovey as Kelly and Eryn Jean Norvill as Sam in the 2012 Q Theatre production at the Seymour Centre. (Photo © Amanda James)

Sam's side. Kelly's side. The truck drivers, their wives or girlfriends or mothers or sons.

Sam's mum, Kelly's mum, Sam's dad, the cop and the counsellor.

Me.

Sam saying,

SAM/AISHA: If this was a TV show.

KELLY: A movie.

SAM: A music clip. We'd be two mad chicks in fast cars burning up the highway, hair flying,

KELLY: Music blaring,

SAM/KELLY: Getting faster and faster and faster,

SAM: Hear us coming?

KELLY: See us coming, how fast / we're racing up the road.

SAM: We're racing up the road.

AISHA: Then there's something there.

KELLY: What is it?

SAM: It's in the way.

AISHA: They see it too late. They swerve, they lose control.

SAM: Our speeding cars don't slow, they scrape each other,

AISHA: Metal hits metal then the dust, the sparks,

KELLY: We skid away from the road, the twist crash hit thud of the cars and / we roll.

SAM: We roll /

KELLY: Brakes gasp /

SAM: Glass rains /

KELLY: Horns blare /

SAM: Thud,

KELLY: Thud,

KELLY/AISHA/SAM: Thud.

AISHA: Then nothing.

> *Pause.*

KELLY: Nothing.

SAM: Just like in a movie.

Then.

KELLY: And now.

AISHA: Then. Before it happened. Kelly and Sam shared everything,

KELLY: Socks,

SAM: Earphones,

KELLY: Leotards,

SAM: Maths, Home-Ec, a sim card,

KELLY: Sausage rolls, diet cokes.

SAM: Shared every day.

KELLY: Texted, facebooked every night.

AISHA: Now. Kelly doesn't speak to Sam. Kelly hardly speaks at all. You can split most things into halves. Movies, hours, oranges, cupcakes.

Friendships don't stand up so well.

> *We hear flies swarming.*

Now. Just after it happened.

Kelly in the waiting room.

KELLY: Chairs hard, condoms in a bucket. Smell antiseptic. Poster of a girl on the wall with cracks all over her face, some message about getting off heroin but she's a model. Her bruises are fake.

    KELLY *tips the remaining water onto the inside of her arm.*

AISHA: She watches / a drop of water run down her arm.

KELLY: A drop of water run down my arm and stop on the vein I'd use if I was a junkie. A little bit blue.

AISHA: Footsteps, high heels up and down the corridor.

KELLY: Woman at the door. She looks at me but doesn't smile. Says:

JOSIE: Hello Kelly, I'm Josie. Would you like to come with me?

KELLY: A little room with a hospital bed and a desk and more posters on the walls. What is it with the people in those posters?

JOSIE: I'm a doctor:

KELLY: She says, asks /

JOSIE: Why are you here today then? / Fly circles around the room.

KELLY: Fly circles around the room.

    Pause.

Clock on the wall.

Tick.

SAM: Tock. / On the clock

KELLY: On the clock. And the party won't / stop

SAM: Stop /

JOSIE: What? Why are you here today?

KELLY: Um… I think there is something wrong down there.

JOSIE: Down there?

KELLY: Want to check it's okay that I haven't got… I want to / get tested

JOSIE: Get tested?

KELLY: Yes.

    KELLY *and* SAM *look at each other and laugh.*

Then.

SAM: Truth?

KELLY: Dare.

SAM: No. Truth. The sexiest bit on a man.

KELLY: Easy. Adam's apples.

    SAM *laughs hysterically.*

SAM: Adam's apples?
KELLY: Yeah.

> KELLY *looks away.*

SAM: Now.

I sit in a shit suburb in an even shittier demountable, next to some counsellor. She looks at me weird. Like she's made it and her life's all sorted. All she does is counselling. Room stinks and the tin walls crack. Fly crawls up her thigh. We're meat in an oven her and me, she's yesterday's left too long. Dried up, grissled.

> MICHELLE *stares at* SAM *and smiles. Waits for her to speak. After a time.*

MICHELLE: How shall we start?

> SAM *shrugs.*

Why don't you tell me why you are here today?

SAM: Don't you know already?
Fly on your face—it's probably laying eggs on you don't you want to brush it off?

> MICHELLE *brushes the fly away.*

It comes straight back sits on her like she's a cow shit, a talking cow shit saying:

MICHELLE: I'd like to hear it from you.
SAM: Mum made me come. And the school, after it happened they said if I want to stay on then I had to see you.
MICHELLE: Do you want to be here today?
SAM: What do you reckon?
MICHELLE: You seem angry, Sam.
SAM: I am angry. Everyone I know thinks I am a cock crazed slut.
MICHELLE: And what do you think?

> SAM *laughs.*

SAM: Good one.
MICHELLE: Would you like to talk about what happened?
SAM: Camera on me for a long time and then, snap, I tear the singlet

off the truckie, run my index finger down his washboard abs, hear him suck in breath, say my line. Nothing can touch us now you know /

MICHELLE: What about your friend? The girl who /

SAM: My friend? / We aren't speaking.

KELLY: We aren't speaking.

SAM: Not a word.

KELLY/SAM: I hate her / She hates me.

KELLY: She did this to me. It's her fault.

SAM: She hates me. It was her idea.

KELLY: Josie looks at me doesn't smile or nothing just asks.

JOSIE: Has something happened that makes you think you need to be tested?

KELLY:

JOSIE: You can say. No need to be embarrassed. Really.

Have you engaged in oral sex?

Penetrative sex?

Was it protected or unprotected?

Kelly?

KELLY:

JOSIE: With one partner? Or more?

KELLY *looks disgusted.*

It's important we get to the facts. When you say you used protection can you tell me what you used.

KELLY:

JOSIE: When did you last have your period?

KELLY: I'm not pregnant. That's not why I am here.

JOSIE: Any stinging or pain? Discharge, any / blood?

KELLY: Blood. Just a bit of blood,

JOSIE: Not /

KELLY: No, not my period.

Something milky. / Discharge.

JOSIE: Discharge. Does / it sting?

KELLY: It stings. A bit. Not all the time.

Looked it up online. Can you fix it?

Can you? Fix it?

Truth?

SAM: Dare.

KELLY: No. Truth.

SAM: Okay. Adam's apples.

> SAM *laughs hysterically.*

KELLY: You bitch.

> KELLY *looks away.*

JOSIE: How old are you?

KELLY/SAM: Fourteen.

SAM: She got in first. Dumped me on facebook. I sent her messages and shit and she barred me.

JOSIE: Have you spoken to someone about this?

SAM/KELLY: Everyone knows.

SAM: She's left school.

JOSIE: But I mean…

KELLY: No.

I just need you to fix it.

> KELLY *and* SAM *sit silent at the picnic table. We see two flies projected, close up, hear swarming.*

Double dare.

SAM: Double dick dare.

KELLY: Double dog dick dare.

SAM: Yuck!

KELLY: Okay then… truth.

AISHA: After it happens the things people say online, names they get called and the jokes. How fast they start. Kelly and Sam. How quick things changed.

Not like how it was. / Then

SAM/KELLY: Then. One year ago.

AISHA: I've just arrived. My first day of school. Kelly's assigned to me by Mrs. Spratt and she drags me about for the morning /

KELLY: Computer room but none of them work, bubblers, canteen—

watch the scabs, smoker's toilet, music room—watch Mr Moxham—
he's a pedo—gets girls to stay back after class and 'sing', lockers,
bin,

Bell rings.

recess. Suppose you want to sit with us.
AISHA: Okay.
KELLY: I'm gonna get a sausage roll.

I hang with Sam.

She's going out with Trent.

That's Trent over there. You think he's hot?

AISHA: Doesn't she sit with him?
KELLY: Na. He's a lad.
AISHA: A lad?
KELLY: Yeah. See their hair?

Lads hang there, we stay here.

AISHA: There's nowhere to sit here.
KELLY: Na. Sucks. Gotta be quick to get somewhere good at the start of
the year. We weren't so this is it.
AISHA: A dusty square of ground with a bin and a cross fire of balls.
KELLY: Stinking hot in summer and now… freeze your tits off once you
grow 'em. Your mum have big tits?
AISHA: What? Why are you asking me that?
KELLY: Just wondered. Mine doesn't.
AISHA: Have you got a boyfriend?
KELLY: Yeah.

Na. Do you?

She offers her sausage roll.

Want a bite?
AISHA: Why'd you ask me that before / about…
KELLY: Tits? You need them that's all. To get one.

SAM *enters catches a ball in mid flight.*

SAM: Want it? Want it? Then come and get it spastic! Dare ya.
Ha! Didn't think ya would.

She sees KELLY*'s sausage roll and makes a face.*

You know how they make sausage rolls? They get the old animals and push them into a tunnel with a blender at the end. You're probably eating pig prick and cat arse.

Trent's a dickhead, sent me a picture of his ugly nipple. Not erect or nothing.

KELLY: This is Aisha.
SAM: She hanging with us?
KELLY: That okay?

SAM *catches another ball. Hides it down her top.*

SAM: Come and get it you fucktard.

He won't.

She throws it back.

Where you from?

AISHA: St Mary's.
SAM: I meant before that.
AISHA: Bangalore. Have you been there?
SAM: Why would I go to Bangalore Curry?
KELLY: Don't call her Curry. You like being called Curry?
AISHA: No.
KELLY: See.
SAM: Well, I don't like being asked shit.

You eating pig too? Aren't you Muslim?

AISHA: No.
KELLY: Don't worry about her. She gets this way. Showing off. Like the whole school's paparazzi. Play along.
SAM: Is that what you do?

She hanging with us?
KELLY: Sam!
SAM: Just she needs to know how long we've been BFs. I met Kelly when I was six.

We're there for each other like, you know, really there. I was there for you when your dad left, wasn't I, Kel?

KELLY: Yeah.

SAM: See? Heard from him Kel?

KELLY:

AISHA: How did you two meet?

KELLY: We did Jazz.

SAM: Dance world is full of stuck up bitches.

KELLY: We were in the same classes in primary.

SAM: Kelly was the first girl at school to get her /

KELLY: Sam /

SAM: Period.

KELLY: Sam, shut up.

SAM: What Kel? You were. It happened just as they brought the lunch orders in. Pies and sauce and then blood all over the chair everyone thought she'd pissed her pants 'cause we didn't know what a period looked like.

The class goes quiet and Miss King puts on a pair of rubber gloves, pushes Kelly out the door to go to sick bay.

KELLY: Yeah thanks for that Sam.

SAM: Curry don't care do you Curry?

KELLY: Don't call her that.

>   SAM *gets a text.*

SAM: Sorry Asia.

KELLY/AISHA: Aisha.

>   SAM *checks her message.*

SAM: Trent wants to make it even, see my nipple.

KELLY: He's just there. Why don't you…

SAM: Na fuck him. I'm not sending nothing. Treat Trent mean. Keep Trent Keen.

KELLY: Our friend Nat left last term. Miss her.

SAM: The three of us were the skanks.

AISHA: The skanks?

KELLY: That was my idea.

SAM: No it wasn't.

KELLY: Bitch you know it was.

SAM: Whatever.

KELLY: The skanks.

Combination of our initials. Sam's name, my name and Nat's name.

SAM: An anagram.

KELLY: An acronym.

SAM: Whatever.

KELLY: Sam Kilbourne, Natalie Archer and Kelly Stoner.

SAM/KELLY: The skanks.

KELLY: Like a gang name or something. We had a tag 'n' shit.

SAM: We were gonna be a pop group.

KELLY: Real elegant like Pussycat Dolls but hotter.

SAM: Much fucking hotter.

KELLY: The Skanks.

SAM: Movie with the same name.

SAM/KELLY: SKANKS.

KELLY: Yeah.

SAM: Yeah. But.

KELLY: Nat left.

SAM: Always fucks up bands when one of the girls leaves.

AISHA: Skanks?

SAM: It was only a name.

KELLY: Yeah, we're not really skanks, it was just like 'self deprecating'.

AISHA: What's a skank?

SAM *and* KELLY *look at each other.*

SAM: Don't you have skanks in Bangalore?

Going to talk to Trent.

She goes.

KELLY: It was the three of us. A gang. Hung out did everything. Planned shit together like formals and schoolies. Then Nat moved. To Narrabeen. She said *I'll come back every weekend to visit.*

The AN gone out of skanks.

SKKS. That's what was left.

Doesn't spell shit. And who'd come back here?

AISHA: You don't like it here?

KELLY: Just off the boat. You'll find out.

> KELLY *leaves* AISHA. *We see a cockroach projected, close up.*

AISHA: Then.

Before we leave I spend time looking at pictures of kangaroos and beaches, lifesavers, girls in bikinis… Richarne, my brother, sad because he does not want to leave. But we are leaving and I am telling him it will be better. We can be anything there. Promise my friends I'll make films, upload them so they can see who I become.

Film the view landing, the red brick houses, the sparkling harbour—we even see the white sails of the Opera House as the plane comes down through cloud.

Brown family everyone else seems white.

Film the train ride to the city and then St Mary's. Count the stops. Lose count of the stops.

Two guys behind us on the train talk about a gang that attacked some kid, bashed till he died.

Dad tells me to stop filming to get ready to get off, that we need to get off at the next stop.

We get off the train. We look out on St Mary's. A tattoo shop and an empty bus idling. A boy sits on a bike and smokes. His long hair waves in the wind.

> SAM *alone with her iPod sits at the picnic table and sings to herself.*

KELLY/AISHA/SAM: Now.

KELLY: Josie takes blood.

JOSIE: Won't take long, look away.

KELLY: Needle in my arm. My blood in tubes with coloured lids, cotton wool and a bandaid on my arm.

JOSIE: You need to make an appointment, come back in a week for the results. You have the symptoms now so… / Chlamydia.

KELLY: Chlamydia.

JOSIE: This is serious Kelly. You know that don't you?

KELLY: Yes.

JOSIE: Are you still in contact with the boy, the man. Are you in touch with him?

KELLY: She puts a little sticker on a container of my blood. Yes.

JOSIE: Then you should /

KELLY: I mean. No. I'm not. She pushes my blood into a bag, presses the seal together and then removes her plastic gloves.

JOSIE: If you can find a way to let him know Kelly because the infection /

KELLY: But I'll be alright? The tablets / will…

JOSIE: Will treat the infection but you won't know all the results for six months Kelly.

KELLY: You mean for… ?

JOSIE: HIV. Yes.

KELLY: Six months?

We see the film AISHA *made of a slow-dying cockroach.*

AISHA: Then

Our new house. Cockroaches scuttling and the smell of stale cigarettes. Incense burning all the time because of the smell. The look on my mother's face as she moves about cleaning each room shaking her head and I say *what Ma?*

My brother and I walk to the main street past the Hillsong Church that doesn't look anything like a church to me. We stop to see if we can hear the hillsongs but we can't.

Police cars cruise up and down the street and the barber waits, sits in his chair and stares at us.

Bakery. Cakes with bright yellow icing.

Men in bright yellow shirts.

That boy we saw on the first day rides past on his rusty bike.

A reptile shop. Supplies for snakes and spiders. A giant beetle in a glass tank touches its feelers together and crawls across a toilet roll. We stare at it and the guy laughs and tells us it is a cockroach from Queensland.

Then Dad's in the street. Worried. Says he didn't know where we'd gone and we need to come home it's getting dark. We should not be out alone.

I film this place. Cold wind blowing. You don't see it when you watch it on screen but the wind coming from the mountains is cold / now.

SAM: Now.

Back at the counsellor's and she's looking at me like I'm just gonna split, like an orange and let all the juice run out just 'cause she asked how it all started like I'm gonna piece it all together for her.

I'm not.

MICHELLE: Would you like some water?

SAM *shrugs.*

SAM: We both look out the window. The car park with the barbed wire fence. The street with the red brick houses. The garbage men and the garbage truck, garbage spewing out of everything.

You like living here?

MICHELLE: Good a place as any.

SAM: I hate it. Bogans everywhere. Can't wait to get out.

MICHELLE *sighs.*

She fiddles with her ugly bracelet and then she looks at my hands.

MICHELLE: I like your ring. Where did you get it?

SAM *shrugs.*

SAM: Folder with my first name on it and a number. Sam 74302.

Why should I speak, not under oath or nothing.

Then she starts. Like she is trying to wear me down in the heat of the room if she can't peel me like an orange she'll bash me against the wall until answers bleed out from me. Questions. One after the other after the other.

MICHELLE: How do you do at school?

SAM: *What is your favourite subject?*

MICHELLE: Do you have a part time job?

SAM: *What do you like to do on the weekends?*

MICHELLE: Someone special in your life? A boyfriend? A girlfriend?

SAM: After she says that she laughs like god knows what. She sounds so stupid laughing at her own question maybe she's lezzo. Sweat spreading from her armpits to the edge of her ugly fucking sagging tits.

MICHELLE: What is your secret talent Sam?

SAM: Do I have a favourite teacher someone I can talk to.

   What I'd like to do when I finish / school

MICHELLE: school /

SAM: Where do I get my / hair done

MICHELLE: hair done /

SAM: How long have I had my / ears pierced

MICHELLE: ears pierced /

SAM: where did I get / that bag

MICHELLE: that bag /

SAM/MICHELLE: the shoes, the iPod

SAM: what am I listening to / do I like music?

MICHELLE: do you like music?

> MICHELLE*'s phone rings. It's a very uncool tone and* SAM *rolls her eyes.*

MICHELLE: Won't be a sec.

SAM: Don't care if you take two years.

MICHELLE: I'm at work Chante.

SAM: *I'm at work Chante.*

MICHELLE: Why have you come home from school? Sick? What's that noise in the background?

I thought you said you were sick. I told you he wasn't… I said he wasn't allowed to be there. The school'll ring me and then what will I say? I'm with a client. I'll call you later. Pick up the phone Chante or… Alright.

Sorry. Sam.

> SAM *shrugs.*

So how are things with Mum and Dad?

What are you thinking?

SAM: What am I thinking?

I say I'm thinking about my first boyfriend.

MICHELLE: Would you like to tell me about that?

SAM: No.

I'm not telling her this.

Trent and I met outside the piercing place. Him alone, just about to have a piercing done. I walk up to him and say what you getting done and he says lip and he asks me if I can stay with him. 'Cause he's scared. I say I'll stay but I don't want to watch the needle go through.

When he comes out pierced, looks hot but he's a bit pale. I tell him maybe he should have a pie or something but he says no, to follow him. He takes me around the side of the Coles delivery docks where they smoke near all the rotten fruit and I look at it, at his lip. Ask does it hurt?

He kisses me.

I don't want to talk about it.

> *We hear teeny pop music.* SAM *dances.* KELLY *comes in with a few Vodka Cruisers.* SAM *shows* KELLY *a text she has got from* TRENT. *They laugh. They take a photograph and send it back. They scull Cruisers.*

AISHA: Then. Saturday night, just getting dark.

Mum and I walk down our street, Mum asks who Kelly is and why a girl I hardly know would invite me to a slumber party, there's this dog. From nowhere this dog. Teeth and barking and it jumps at us, Mum reaches for my hand, grips it, stands between me and the dog. Mum protects me even though she is scared. She stares at the dog like it's some demon. Then this old man appears, grabs it by the collar.

We get to Kelly's door. Me with a bottle of creaming soda.

Mum behind me. Music inside and shrieking.

KELLY: Oh my fucking god!
AISHA: The door flies open /
KELLY: We found a picture of Justin Beiber nude online
SAM: He hasn't got pubes.
AISHA: Then them both looking at me and my mum.
KELLY: Hello.

AISHA: This is my mum. Mum, this is Sam and Kelly.

SAM/KELLY: The skanks.

AISHA: Mum shuffles her feet, pokes me in the back as a prompt. My mum wants to meet yours. She says she needs to meet her or I can't…

KELLY: MUM!

MUM!

She's with Bruce.

AISHA: Hear the TV get turned down, then footsteps. Kelly's mum comes to the door, wears a porn star t-shirt, I hope Mum doesn't read it, what it says.

CHARMAINE: I'm Charmaine.

AISHA: She's younger than my mum but looks tired. Dark rings under her eyes.

She doesn't invite mum in.

Leads her out the front.

They're next to one of the cars that sits like a big fish in the long grass.

Whose cars are those?

KELLY: They were Dad's.

SAM: Look at your mum, what's she saying?

SAM *and* KELLY *laugh,* AISHA *cringes.*

AISHA: She's shaking her head a little and looking down at her feet.

CHARMAINE: Go on girls, inside.

AISHA: Mum calls me over and kisses me, whispers to call her if… doesn't matter what time. Then Kelly and Sam pull me inside, slam the door.

Why'd you say the skanks thing?

KELLY: Joke.

SAM: Irony.

KELLY: Yeah.

SAM: Like when wogs call themselves wogs.

KELLY: Or fags.

SAM: Jocks.

KELLY: Geeks.

AISHA: Mum doesn't get irony.

We watch youtube. Some prank film with school boys and snakes.

SAM/KELLY/AISHA: Look at the snake!

KELLY: Bruce at the door tells us /

BRUCE: Keep it down.

KELLY: [*under her breath*] Fuck off.

BRUCE: What did you just say?

KELLY: Nothing.

SAM: He live here now?

KELLY: He's such a loser.

SAM: And ugly as.

KELLY: Mum doesn't even like him he's just a rebound fuck. She still calls Love Song Dedications about Dad.

AISHA: On youtube, some girl who didn't know she was pregnant gives birth to twins in a mall in America.

SAM: I'm gonna be a film star.

KELLY: Like her?

SAM: As if!

KELLY: You don't even do Drama.

SAM: So? We should have done a skank film. With Nat. In that abandoned motel. Uploaded it. Could have been a slasher film, all the ugly girls die first then the hot killer dude comes after me.

KELLY: Why are you last?

SAM: I wonder.

AISHA: Why is it always about being hot for a guy?

SAM: You serious?

AISHA: Yeah.

> SAM *and* KELLY *pass a look.*

KELLY: Want a Cruiser Aisha?

SAM: Have one it's okay.

AISHA: No. I'm alright.

KELLY: Mum got them for us. Go on.

> AISHA *takes one.*

AISHA: And we're back online hunting Justin Beiber's penis but it isn't him at all, hair all wrong.

SAM: What's your favourite movie Aisha?

KELLY: Ours is *Pretty Woman*. It's totally retro but /

SAM: Let's watch it.

KELLY: Let's get pizza.

AISHA: In the slow bits of the film we talk about / prostitutes.

SAM/KELLY: Prostitutes.

KELLY: You tell the story of your brother's mate, Dario. The ugly one. How he was still a virgin and everyone knew 'cause he was fat and ugly and how on his eighteenth they took him up to the industrial and told him they'd all put in. Pay for him to lose it that night, so he could be happy.

SAM: They cruise along, all of them in a car and let him pick whatever one he wants.

And he picks one that looks okay outside the car but once they get her inside she stinks and when she speaks she sounds rough as and she makes a joke that isn't even funny and smiles and she's missing a tooth right in the front but it's too late then 'cause Dario's picked and he's agreed—that was the deal. Once he's chosen no piking. He has to go through with it.

So they drive him to the park. All his mates get out of the car and leave him in the back with / the hooker.

KELLY/AISHA: The hooker.

SAM: His mates sit at a picnic table drinking beer but they can see he's just sitting in the car next to the hooker not doing nothing but talking.

And so they go back and tell him they didn't pay for him to talk to her, to get a move on and fuck her. They make him start while they watch. They tell her *go down on him*. They get him to grab her head and push it down on his cock, *fuck her face* they yell and they film it, his hands pushing down her head, him pushing her legs up, her high heels tapping the back of the window near the bulldogs sticker. Then they open the back door and film him doing it to her.

KELLY: Poor chick.

SAM: You reckon?

KELLY: Yeah.

SAM: She got paid. So what?

KELLY: But…

> *Pause.*

What would it feel like to make money from sex?

SAM: It'd be ok.

KELLY/AISHA: No.

SAM: It would. You could be in control of it.

KELLY: How? Like Dario with that chick?

SAM: Not like that. If I did it I'd be classy.

AISHA: Like Julia Roberts?

SAM: Guys are just gagging for it and you can hold back or you can make them cum in three minutes flat for what…

KELLY: The money. We could afford to buy whatever shit we wanted, clothes, sunglasses

SAM: Cocktails, concert tickets…

KELLY: Go into the city on weekends.

SAM: How much would you charge?

KELLY: Twenty bucks?

SAM/AISHA: Twenty bucks?

KELLY: I don't know… forty?

SAM: Better than selling donuts.

KELLY: I guess.

SAM: Easier.

KELLY: What would you call yourself?

SAM: I'd be Princess.

KELLY: Princess who?

SAM: Just Princess… what about you?

KELLY: Chilli. Hot Chilli.

SAM: Sick! What about you Aish?

AISHA: I don't know.

SAM: Oh come on.

AISHA: I don't know.

SAM: Jai hoe.

> *Knock at the door.*

ALL: Pizza!

SAM: Hope the pizza dude's hot.

KELLY: He's not. He's all pimpled. Looks worried.

SAM: I play a trick on him.

Sorry but we didn't order pizza.

AISHA: He looks at the docket over and over again until Sam bursts out laughing.

SAM: Got ya!

KELLY: Pay him./

SAM: Slam the door in his face.

AISHA: That was mean.

SAM: He's a pizza guy. So what?

AISHA: And later, watching Channel V, Katy Perry licking ice creams and popsicles Sam says:

SAM: Aisha.

AISHA: What?

SAM: Your last name is / Nadu right?

AISHA: Nadu right.

SAM: You have the same initials as Nat did. Nat Archer. Aisha Nadu. Just reverse.

AISHA: Kelly rolls off the couch and jumps up on the coffee table says:

KELLY: Oh my fucking god!

AISHA: And we all look at each other, cold pizza sweats, music blares, heater full blast and Sam says it.

SAM: S-K-A-N-K-S. We can be the skanks again.

We see a movie made that night made by AISHA. KELLY *and* SAM *scull Cruisers. They dance and scream on top of a rusty car.*

AISHA *alone.*

AISHA: Then.

Dad in a taxi. His other job.

I say to him that's not why we came here, Mum puts a box of tissues out for the passengers says /

INDHU: It's just for a little while. Until…

AISHA: Dad's tying Ganesh to the mirror.

INDHU: For protection.

AISHA: Protection for who? And Mum says /

INDHU: Everyone needs protection.

AISHA: Dad waves to us as he drives off, wet stains in the armpits of his blue uniform.

How will Ganesh protect Dad, Mum? If some guy gets in the car and threatens Dad with a knife what's Ganesh going to do? Wave a rat at him?

INDHU *shakes her head.*

INDHU: You are not to say those things.
AISHA: You mean things that are / true?
SAM: Truth.
INDHU: Things that show no respect.
KELLY: Dare.
INDHU: Things that make you sound like…
SAM/KELLY: Double dog dick dare.
INDHU: Go inside and study.

AISHA *goes.*

We hear flies.

SAM: Then.
KELLY: Us.
SAM/KELLY: Tuesday. Recess.
KELLY: People saying Trent got with Brittany.
SAM: Which Brittany?
KELLY: The slutty faced one who works at Boost.
SAM: That dog. Who'd touch her?
KELLY: Um, Trent. And I heard Trent emailed Darren pictures of your tits.
SAM: Darren?
KELLY: Yeah.
SAM: Hot Darren or rat-tail Darren.
KELLY: Rat-tail.
SAM: Yuck.
KELLY: Stop sending Trent shit.

You can trace it you know. Phone companies keep records.

SAM: They do not.
KELLY: They do.

SAM: So what? Like have you seen how many tits are online? Who's gonna be trawling through all of them to find mine Kelly? Some old pedo at Vodafone?

KELLY: Dump him.

SAM: I will. But… I like him. He's in Year Ten and…

KELLY: He treats you like a whore.

SAM: He's alright.

KELLY: It's my job. Like as your best friend and all to watch out for you.

SAM: Yeah yeah.

KELLY: We made that deal like what they said in class. Look out for your mates. Protect them. Talk. And if something's going wrong /

SAM: Don't tell me what to do. I can make my own decisions.

KELLY: Then…

SAM: Don't want to be single.

KELLY: There's other guys.

SAM: I love him.

KELLY: Does he love you?

Does he?

SAM: He says he does.

KELLY: When?

SAM: Kel…

KELLY: What? When you and Trent /

SAM: What?

KELLY: Fuck.

SAM: We do not fuck.

KELLY: What do you do then? Make love?

They laugh.

Do you use rubbers?

SAM: Yes.

KELLY: Do you?

SAM: Gonna go on the pill.

Don't look at me like that. Hey how's this? Trent reckons we should have a threesome.

KELLY: That's bullshit.

SAM: You jealous?

KELLY: A threesome? What you want to do that for?

SAM: *What you want to do that for?*

KELLY: Don't be a bitch.

SAM: Guys love it, spice shit up. You know, like meet someone at a party, show each other your junk…

KELLY: A girl?

SAM: As if Trent'd do it with a guy.

KELLY: So you'd…

SAM: Yeah.

KELLY: Do you even like /

SAM: It's not about that Kelly.

Feel left out? Get a boyfriend.

KELLY: Yeah, easy.

SAM: You're not that bad.

Don't know why you'd bother. Teenage boys are hopeless, not like in the movies. When Trent and I first started, he kissed like a salmon.

He's more sensual now.

KELLY: What? Like a shark?

SAM: Funny. Someone older might have their own place.

KELLY: What do you mean?

SAM: With school boys there's nowhere to do it. Like I can hardly just come home and say oh hey Mum and Dad Trent's here and he's really horny and I'll be out for dinner in a minute, I just got to give him head.

Trent wants to do it everywhere.

KELLY: Like where?

SAM: You know.

KELLY: No.

SAM: Like he took me into the disabled toilets at Westfield once said *get down on your knees and suck my cock.*

KELLY: At Westfield?

SAM: Imagine it. Some cripple needs a shit and… you know… I didn't want to. Not there. It always leads to the same thing with Trent. And I don't want to…

Down on your knees bitch and suck. Like we are in some porno.

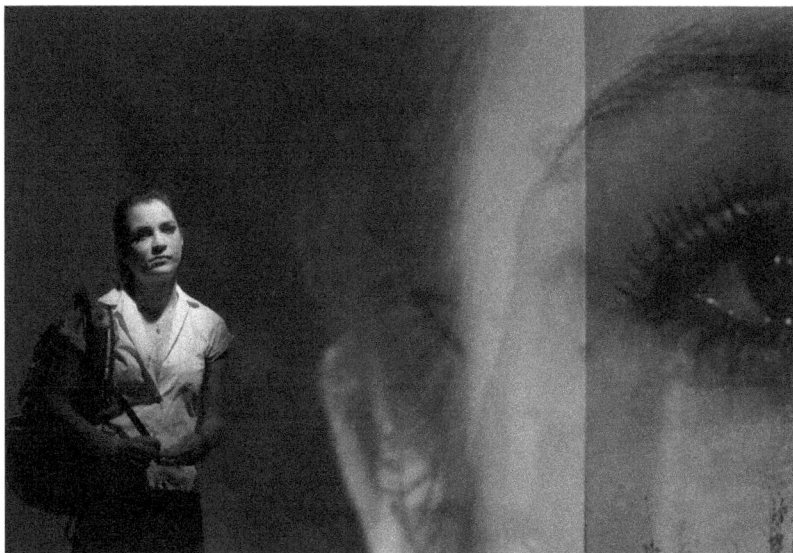

Jessica Tovey as Kelly in the 2012 Q Theatre production at the Seymour Centre. (Photo © Amanda James)

Says stuff, swears and shit. He spat on me.

KELLY *looks shocked.*

SAM: And I spat back. In his eye and I told him not to say shit like that again and if he did /

KELLY: I don't know why you stay with him.

We hear truck drivers on a CB, everyday banter with static and interference. KELLY *returns to the picnic table. Waits with a plastic cup of water.*

KELLY: Now.

In the clinic waiting room.

Fluorescent lights off, me alone.

Flick through a magazine pictures of the Kardashians, tennis players, soapie stars and their ugly looking kids, nurse passes, smiles, flicks the light on says: /

NURSE: You'll go blind if you read in the dark love.

KELLY: Smell perfume, then these two women walk in.

Look real glamorous at first, but then under the light…

One of them is in pink but it's spattered with blood, tattoo of a leopard on her calf, long bleached hair, split ends.

Other one's skinny and isn't in much at all. Her body shakes and she's crying. Her eyes red and her head shakes, back and forth she's saying / I can't believe he did that to me,

SEX WORKER: I can't believe he did that to me—

KELLY: Her friend reaches out to hold her hand and I see bruises up her skinny arms.

She looks at me and opens her mouth, is about to say something, I can see her rotten teeth.

Josie comes to the door, looks at them, then at me,

JOSIE: Kelly.

KELLY: I look back at those two women under the flicking light.

JOSIE: What did she say to you?

KELLY: Is she okay?

Her friend… Are they prostitutes?

JOSIE: We don't use that term here Kelly. Sex workers.

How are you today?

KELLY: It's cleared up.

JOSIE: Good. Most of the tests are back. There was an infection. It should be fine now but I'd like to check. Take off your pants and lie back on the bed.

KELLY: I hate this. Pants down, I lie on that bed and stare up at the ceiling.

The sex worker's shouting something down the hall like she's gone crazy.

JOSIE: Okay. Looks fine Kelly. But you know that / there is still the window period.

KELLY: There is still the window period. Yes.

JOSIE: I'd like you to talk to the councellor.

KELLY: Don't want to.

JOSIE: Why is that?

KELLY: Just don't.

JOSIE: You are under the age of consent Kelly. You could /

KELLY: What? Report them?

JOSIE: Yes. It's illegal. You could talk to the police or /

KELLY: I wasn't raped. I wasn't drunk or out of control. I just did it. They had money and I took it. I just let them do it. And I don't want to talk to anyone else about it.

Can I go?

> KELLY *now sits in front of the television staring. We hear some mindless American talk show which morphs into loud white noise.*

SAM: Then

AISHA: In the middle of Maths

KELLY: Miss going on about surds and indices then / BANG.

SAM/AISHA: BANG.

KELLY: An explosion outside. / Something's happened.

SAM/AISHA: Something's happened.

AISHA: Like what happened on the trains.

KELLY: Like the World Trade Towers.

SAM: Like an action movie, extras catch alight and burn alive.

SAM/KELLY: Something's happened.

AISHA: No bell ringing, no announcement, nothing at all.

SAM: And you can see on Miss' face she wants to find out what just blew up /

KELLY: We just walk, calm from the classroom towards the hill that overlooks the road.

SAM/KELLY/AISHA: Truck on its side.

SAM: Driver stands in the dirt by the side of the road, shakes his head.

AISHA: Skid marks, wheels spin.

KELLY: Dead dog in a pool of blood.

SAM: One less mutt to scare you Aish.

AISHA: Back doors of the truck open and boxes everywhere.

KELLY: It's a Cadbury truck!

SAM/KELLY/AISHA: Chocolate.

SAM: OMG. Can we…

KELLY: Miss mouth wide open, thinks the same thing as us you can see but /

SAM: Then Miss Rowse is behind us yelling /

ROWSE: Go back to class right now, on the double or you can have detention for a term.

SAM: What about Miss, Miss?

KELLY: And then after school.

SAM: Word of the crash spread like Ebola.

Let's go out and watch Kel. Just us two.

KELLY: Dog gone and the truck as well just skid marks on the road.

SAM: Some moron boys from Year Seven fossick on the edge of the highway for chocolate find a couple of smarties, hold them up like nuggets of gold.

KELLY: Wonder if the family know the dog's dead yet?

SAM: Wonder if he'll get sacked.

KELLY: The truckie?

SAM: Yeah.

KELLY: Na. He'll just make up some story.

SAM: When did you find out your parents lie?

KELLY: You serious?

SAM: Yeah. When did you realise?

KELLY: I don't know. Why you asking that?

SAM: Dunno. Just thinking about it. How they tell. How the truck driver tells his boss and his wife and shit.

KELLY: How they tell the kids about the dog.

SAM: No point telling kids that. Why would you tell them their dog got crushed?

Just say chocolate's bad for dogs.

They laugh.

KELLY: Nat's party on the weekend. She sent me a text today.

SAM: She didn't send me one.

KELLY: Facebook?

SAM: Nothing. Not even a fucking poke. Not going to her party. Don't care if her parents have gone away and the whole of her new school is going. Haven't heard from her and I don't give a shit. Fucking stuck up bitch. She thinks she's moved to Summer Bay. Take Aisha with you /

KELLY: Don't /

SAM: She'll film it for her mates back home. Curries must all have boring fucking lives if the best thing they can do is sit around and watch what she's filmed in this dump.

KELLY: She just misses them Sam. Like we miss Nat.

SAM: I don't miss Nat. Take Curry. I'm not going.

Take her stinky mum too. She can look at everyone like they've got / three heads.

AISHA *enters.*

AISHA: Hi.

KELLY: Hi Aish.

SAM: What do you want?

KELLY: Sam!

SAM: What? What do you want Aish?

AISHA: I hang out with you guys.

SAM: We're not guys. We don't have dicks.

KELLY: Sam.

AISHA: What's the problem? Have I done something?

SAM: Suppose Nat's been in touch with you too has she? Saw you two are friends on facebook even though you have never met.

AISHA: *She* asked *me*.

SAM: I bet she did.

AISHA: What was I meant to do? Ignore her?

SAM: You going Saturday night? To Nat's.

AISHA: Not allowed.

SAM: So why should that stop you?

SAM: Do our friendships mean something to you?

AISHA: Yeah.

SAM: Then figure it out.

AISHA *goes.*

KELLY: So you gonna come as well?

SAM: Yeah.

KELLY: Sam. About Aish…

It was you who got her to be a skank.

SAM: Her name started with an A.

KELLY: Yeah.

SAM: And I thought I'd give her a go.

KELLY: Then give her a go.

> SAM *goes.* KELLY *is alone. We hear the following radio conversation.*

MERCER: This is Love Song Dedications and I've got Charmaine on the line. How are you on this chilly night Charmaine?

CHARMAINE: I'm doing alright Richard.

MERCER: You don't sound like you are.

CHARMAINE: No.

MERCER: What's been happening Charmaine?

CHARMAINE: Things have been a bit tough lately Richard.

MERCER: That's not good Charmaine.

CHARMAINE: No it's not.

MERCER: And is there someone out there who could make things better?

CHARMAINE: Yes.

MERCER: You think he might be listening tonight?

CHARMAINE: I don't know.

MERCER/CHARMAINE: You can hope / I can hope.

MERCER: There's always hope.

CHARMAINE: We used to listen to your show together Richard. After we'd had our tea.

MERCER: I'm sure you'll listen together again Charmaine. And if that person out there is listening right now, what would you like to say?

CHARMAINE: I'd like to say I miss you Tom. Nothing is the same now. Without you. We should have tried harder. [*Savage Garden 'Truly Madly Deeply' plays softly.*] We could have spoken about things more and if you come back…

> *We hear* CHARMAINE *break down.* KELLY *goes.*

> AISHA *dances in front of the mirror. She practises moves for the party and sings along.*

> *The music stops.*

INDHU: What sort of party? Who are you going with? Who's going to be there?

AISHA: My brother stops, a shadow in the doorway.

INDHU: Aisha?

AISHA: He stares at me, at what I'm wearing,

INDHU: Aisha?

AISHA: Listens to me lie, goes to his room to sit in the lonesome glow of Call of Duty.

INDHU: You're not wearing that are you?

AISHA: What do you expect me to wear Mum?

R and B music. SAM *and* KELLY *dress provocatively for* NAT*'s party.*

SAM/KELLY: Then.

SAM: We meet up at Kelly's.

KELLY: Mum's got stuff for us for the party

SAM: My mum'd never do that the bitch.

KELLY *holds up UDLs in a shopping bag.*

UDLs?

KELLY: Better than nothing.

SAM *gets a message.*

SAM: Trent wants to see my tits again.

KELLY: He's fully boring. He should shove the camera up his arse.

SAM: Look at what he sent me…

They look at the phone screen and scream. AISHA *arrives.*

KELLY: Where you been?

AISHA: Cross-examination.

KELLY: Did the Hillsong story work?

AISHA: Yep.

SAM: You can't wear that. You need sexifying.

KELLY: I've got shit you can wear. Come on.

Music gets louder. KELLY *and* AISHA *go.* SAM *dances and drinks quickly.*

AISHA *returns dressed in* CHARMAINE*'s porn star t-shirt and a skirt that resembles a napkin.*

SAM: The Bombay Bitch! Photo!

The pose for a photo.

ALL: SKANKS!

SAM: Walk to the station for the five o'clock train.

KELLY: Aisha watches out for her mum.

SAM: She wouldn't recognise you hey?

AISHA: Then just before we go up the steps for the train. Outside the tattoo shop.

> SAM *points.*

SAM: Fuck Aish, it's your mum!

> AISHA *freezes.*

Just kidding.

Frozen curry.

AISHA: You bitch.

SAM: Got ya!

KELLY: And we're off!

AISHA: Train moves closer to the city the distant high rises takes shape singing /

> *The girls sing the chorus of 'We R Who We R' by Ke$ha. They stop singing suddenly. They all drink UDLs and stare.*

KELLY: Girl with a pram. Look.

It's Tatum.

SAM: It's not.

SAM/KELLY: It is.

KELLY: Tatum with her kid.

SAM: She's ignoring us.

KELLY: Maybe we look so hot she doesn't recognise us.

> KELLY *smiles, waves.*

Tatum shows off the kid. What's his name?

TATUM: Bailey.

KELLY: He's fast asleep.

SAM: It's like he's made of plastic.

TATUM: Not when he shits.

KELLY: Kid opens his eyes.

TATUM: It hurt when I had him.

SAM: She tells us she and Jed are happy.

TATUM: He's got an apprenticeship now. I was gonna come back to school but…

KELLY: She doesn't even ask where we're going. Train stops. She gets off.

They watch her leave.

SAM: She used to be real pretty you know.

KELLY: She still looks okay.

SAM: Na. She's fat as fuck.

KELLY: Needs a personal trainer.

SAM: And some decent clothes.

KELLY: Wonder why she called him Bailey?

SAM: She was eyeing off our UDLs.

KELLY: What would it feel like to be pregnant you reckon?

SAM: You'd have to be pretty fucking dumb to have a kid. You know what I'm saying.

AISHA: Some guy in a hoodie stares at the three of us…

SAM: What is this, staring Saturday?

KELLY: Look away.

SAM: Why should I?

KELLY: Easier.

SAM: Why can't he?

KELLY: Let's change carriages.

SAM: The douchebag follows.

KELLY: Stares at Aisha now like he's a spy been sent by her mum.

AISHA: He's not Indian.

KELLY: We've been drinking fast.

SAM: Last UDL. Scull it Aish!

AISHA *sculls.*

KELLY: Change trains.

AISHA/SAM: Wait.

KELLY: Change trains.

AISHA/SAM: Wait.

KELLY: Bus.

AISHA: Walk.

SAM: After three hours we get to the end of Nat's street in Narrabeen.

AISHA: It's colder here. Wind coming from the sea.

KELLY: None of us brought nothing warm.

AISHA: Car drives past and beeps and then... Hear that?

SAM: THE PARTY!

KELLY: Music belts and a girl screams and some guys shouting.

AISHA: Three balloons out the front of number 52. We're here.

SAM/KELLY: Nat screams.

KELLY: Runs up to hug us.

SAM: Smells of vomit and cigarettes and something sweet, musk?

ALL: Took us three hours to get here.

KELLY: People laugh when we tell them that.

AISHA: Some guy called Robbo shouts out:

ROBBO: Did youz hear how long it took for the westie chicks to get here?

KELLY: Nat laughs.

SAM: Rub our noses in it hey? Tell us how much better it is living here /

KELLY: How much better the shops are /

SAM: How much hotter the guys are 'cause they go surfing instead of drive about the streets.

KELLY: People ask how we know Nat.

SAM: Like it's some reunion film and she left St Mary's 20 years ago.

KELLY: And thanks, Sam, you're telling everyone about how we all met. What happened to me in year four, story of blood on the seat in the classroom and no guy goes near me after that wish you wouldn't /

SAM: That dude's hitting on me. Keeps /

KELLY: What?

SAM: Keeps staring at my tits and... can you leave me alone for a bit?

KELLY: What?

SAM: Fuck. You heard! Don't follow me okay?

SAM *makes eyes at the dude and vanishes.*

AISHA: Nat's house has a big garden with palm trees and a view of water.

KELLY: People seem alright.

AISHA: Guys keep giving me drinks.

KELLY: You're drinking a lot Aish.

AISHA: So?

KELLY: Every time I see you you're holding some new drink.

AISHA: Let me have some fun.

KELLY: And the music goes up / it's loud the beat.

AISHA: It's loud the beat like a heart under your feet.

KELLY: Aisha having fun alright she's dancing in the middle of it.

    SAM *comes back.*

SAM: She's dancing like a stripper.

KELLY: Where you been?

SAM: All these guys watching Aisha.

KELLY: It's no wonder 'cause she's really hot wish I could film this for her so she could see how the guys are looking at her wish I could film it so she could send it back to her friends.

SAM: This blond surfer guy looking at Aisha and they're smiling at each other and he's leaning in to kiss her.

KELLY: She's pashing this guy and everyone's cheering.

SAM: She's all over him, people asking where she's from and they're all singing Jai Ho.

KELLY: Music louder someone puts on that song. / Jai Ho, you are my destiny

SAM: *Jai Ho, you are my destiny.*

KELLY: Everyone dancing.

SAM: Chicks doing waterfall.

KELLY: Song ends.

SAM/KELLY: Aisha disappears.

KELLY: Hand on my shoulder. Nat. Drunk. Tells me / she needs to talk.

NAT: I need to talk.

KELLY: We sit in her mum and dad's room on the velvet bedspread, noise from the party everywhere but quiet on the bed.

Nat looks at herself in the mirror and then at me and then a tear runs down her face.

A bottle of vodka between us and she bawls. Nat?

Nat? What's wrong? You can tell me…

But she just sits there crying. Doesn't say a word.

SAM: I come in and see you both. / Seeing Nat crying makes me mad.

KELLY: Seeing Nat crying me with my arm around her makes her say:

SAM: You're fucking sick. You lezzos.

KELLY: Why you always mad at everything Sam? We're just /

AISHA: And outside, I'm grinding and kissing this guy with big lips don't know his name and he's telling me I'm pretty, he's telling me I'm hot and he's asking if it's true what's on my t-shirt.

SAM: Trent sends me a filthy text / he says

AISHA: He says you want another shot, asks if I want to come to another party /

SAM: Trent saying he wishes he was there 'cause he'd tit fuck me /

AISHA: Some mate of his turning twenty-one there'll be cocaine /

SAM: *Want to see my cum around your pretty neck /*

AISHA: Smiles at me asks do you like / blow?

SAM: */ Blow all over your tits babe.*

AISHA: Do I like blow?

SAM: Send him back a pic of my eye.

AISHA: He grins and gets me another drink.

SAM: Send him a pic of my ear and my hand my leg my wrist my elbow /

AISHA: He runs his hand through my hair.

SAM: Send him the pics and then I write a text. I say this is me too Trent.

AISHA: He kisses me. His tongue pushes against mine, soft at first then harder, he licks my ear whispers *I'm Jasper.*

SAM: See the pics of my eyes and ears and hands and my elbows? I'm more than just two tits Trent. I'm /

AISHA: Jasper asks me if I want a shot of tequila. Lick sip suck he says. He's grinning. I lick sip suck. Then I throw up in the bushes. Jasper sees me chuck and leaves. Doesn't say goodbye.

KELLY: Party dying. Look through the front window at a group of guys bursting the balloons out front as they go.

SAM: Guys are such pigs. Beer bottles everywhere.

KELLY: Cigarette burn on the toilet seat.

SAM: Broken chair.

KELLY: Bonsai toppled, dirt spilled in the hall.

SAM: Aisha's phone rings. / Ya mum.

KELLY: Ya mum. Sam's phone rings. Trent.

SAM: / Trent.

SAM/AISHA: Turn it off.

KELLY: Silent. Sam, Nat, Aish and me left.

KELLY: We climb up and sit on Nat's roof. We can see the moon on the sea, two yellow lights twinkle out on the water. Look like /

SAM: Eyes.

AISHA: Apricots.

NAT: Diamonds.

KELLY: Lovers.

SAM: Lovers? How do they look like lovers?

KELLY: They just do… Two lovers sitting there quietly together… you know.

> *The girls laugh then sit on the roof, still, quiet. We hear insects which morph into the sounds of CB radio, a train.*

Train ride back.

No-one speaks for ages then Sam goes up the end of the train to ring Trent. Make up.

AISHA: I get off the train with Kelly. Two ugly guys at the tattoo shop stare.

> *We hear a wolf whistle.*

KELLY/AISHA: Let's run.

AISHA: We run. Stop outside the church. My head.

KELLY: Change back into your Hillsong clothes.

AISHA: Walk up our street, hear the buzz of the big grey power tower that's behind our house in place of a tree, and all the trucks speeding past on the freeway just want to slip in the back door but Dad's out the front, claps his hands, then mum's there asking /

INDHU: How was the church party? What songs did you sing, what did they feed you, were there any nice boys?

AISHA: My head pounds.

INDHU: Did you make some films? Can I see them?

AISHA: I'm tired, show you later.

INDHU: But I told you. We're going to the Guptas' today for a barbeque.

AISHA: The Guptas'?

> AISHA *grimaces.*

SAM: I get off the train and Chelsea Mills is there on the platform that stuck up bitch on her way to dance class. She looks at me like I'm a dog and asks me *you still dancing*? and then she asks *did you hear I won the tap eisteddfod*?

The tap eisteddfod?

Bollywood music crackles.

AISHA: I'm full of aloo gobi and Mrs Gupta's questions. Mum sighs as she asks:

INDHU: Did I tell you I met Shahrukh Khan?

AISHA: We've heard before Mum. What are we walking clichés?

Mum and Mrs Gupta give me the look.

INDHU: Respect young lady. If there is not respect then there is /

AISHA: Yeah? What? I storm off, hide in the bathroom replay last night back in my head. Jasper smiles, dances over to me, his ringlets, his smile, his blue eyes… And this time I don't vomit on the bushes and he doesn't have anywhere else to go. We sit on the rooftop, hold hands stare out at the apricots at sea. Then we kiss.

SAM: Get home and Dad says how was the party Princess? They've been to Bunnings and bought a new leaf blower and a mulcher and… I go straight to my room. Slam the door. Stand in front of the mirror, press play and…

Fuck you Chelsea Mills.

She dances.

KELLY: Get home, Mum sitting on the couch staring at the TV—she couldn't be watching that shit. She smokes and pours a wine from a cask into a coffee cup and she's about to speak only I'm not in the mood. Don't want to hear her.

CHARMAINE: Kel?

KELLY: I walk.

CHARMAINE: Kelly?

KELLY: Go to my room and slam it shut. Lie on my bed, Rihanna on the back of the door, wrapped in an American flag pouts at me.

Turn on the computer, shut the blinds, charge my phone, footsteps in the hallway. Rihanna shakes a little bit as Mum knocks on the door. Mum stands in my doorway crying.

Why you crying? Did Bruce leave you? He's a loser anyway.

CHARMAINE: You need to give him a chance Kelly.

KELLY: I kick off my boot and it hits the wall.

Give him a chance? Did you ask me if he could move in?

CHARMAINE: It's my house Kelly.

KELLY: It's Dad's house.

CHARMAINE: Not anymore. I can do what I like so you better be nice to him.

KELLY: Nice to him? You know what? Bruce is ugly. Not just his face or the way he smells but something inside him is ugly too. Don't you see the way he looks at me? He's like a cockroach come to get whatever scraps he can get from the trash. What does that make you?

CHARMAINE *slaps* KELLY.

SAM: Truth.

KELLY: Neighbour's dog barks.

SAM: Dare.

KELLY: Feel like whacking you back, feel like hitting you hard, feel like reaching and grabbing you and pulling you close to me.

SAM: Double dare.

KELLY: Feel like running.

Look away from you, never want to see you again.

SAM: Truth.

KELLY: I want you dead.

And then calm as anything you say.

CHARMAINE: What would you know?

KELLY: I want you to get out. You're fucking crazy. / What would I know?

CHARMAINE: What would you know?

KELLY: I don't want you in here anymore.

What would I know?

I don't want to see you. I want to run away from you I want another mother.

CHARMAINE: This isn't about you. Not everything is about you Kelly. I know what happened to you but move on. You saw a counsellor. It was years ago

KELLY: Move on?

CHARMAINE: Yes.

KELLY: How can you say that? I was eleven.

CHARMAINE: I know.

KELLY: Do you? 'Cause you act like you forget. And that's when I cry. That's when the carpet swallows me like the sea and I'm scared.

And she looks at me like she doesn't get it but she does.

I wish Dad was here.

The room spinning.

The carpet the sea in a storm, the blinds sharp knives in the wind.

Who have I got?

Who will protect me?

We see images of moths and flies buzzing around a light. We hear CB radio noise, snippets of conversation but nothing intelligible.

AISHA: Then.

Cockroach wakes me up, runs across my mouth, it's in my hair scratching my scalp. Car headlights through the window and I see Mum outside in the cold. She stands on the dirt in her dressing-gown and slippers where Dad says we'll grow grass. She's talking to the tower. She's telling it why we've come here. Part of me wants to put my hand on her shoulder, say what she wants to hear. The other part of me wants to push her over. Mum?

INDHU: You scared me.

AISHA: You scared me. What the fuck are you doing out here freak? I don't get you. You're miserable. You hate it here but you don't make an effort to fit in. All you do besides sit at home is visit the Guptas.

Why did you bring us here? You'll never fit in and then I'll never fit in and…

INDHU: Aisha.

AISHA: She reaches out, tries to hold my hand. And I laugh at her and walk away.

AISHA goes.

Daylight.

SAM *then* KELLY.

SAM: Then.

KELLY: The mall after school.

SAM: The food court near the donut shop, anything to avoid going home.

AISHA *enters.*

AISHA: I film the boys, all their haircuts. Them coming in and out of the toilets 'cause they're checking their hair, the colours, the tips, the shape.

KELLY: Faggots the lot of them. Just don't know it yet.

AISHA: This boy with beautiful skin. Noah from Samoa.

KELLY: He plays football.

SAM: Are they bitch tits or pecs?

AISHA: Noah from Samoa smiles at me when I look.

KELLY: Noah from Samoa's watching you, whoooo.

AISHA: Noah has really curly hair he's trying to make straight. He looks serious not rough like some of his mates.

Noah buys a bag of donuts and shares them with his mates.

SAM: Bitch tits, see?

AISHA: I see him every day after school at the food court. If I'm sly I can catch him on film and take it home and watch it. I lie on my bed and imagine what it would be like to dance with Noah. Lie on my bed and imagine what it would be like dancing to a slow song and then move in to kiss him.

Mum comes in. She sits next to me on the bed gives me a look.

INDHU: Something weighs on me.

AISHA: She asks me about the day when we met Kelly's mum. She asks about Sam and Kelly. Then she says /

INDHU: I've been on the internet. I want to know why those girls call themselves the skanks. Do you know what it means?

AISHA: Then she stops talking and stares at me.

INDHU: Are you going to go back to church? Maybe you could meet other girls there.

AISHA: She picks up my phone. The phone that's made all the films. Films of us, when we got here when I knew no-one else. Films of school, of the skanks in the playground, at Westfield, the night at Kelly's and the party at Nat's.

INDHU: When did you take this photo?

AISHA: It was… at a party.

INDHU: A party? What party? Where was that party and when did you go?

AISHA: Dad comes home. He looks tired now doesn't smile like he did. Mum shows him the photo on the phone. Says:

INDHU: Look at your daughter, what your daughter is becoming.

AISHA: And I say what do you mean by that Mum?

My father looks at the photo, then at me, then at my mother.
He says

INDHU/AISHA: *My daughter is becoming a woman.*

We hear flies and the traffic on the highway.

SAM: Then

Week after Nat's party, I'm at school and this little cow in year seven starts slutting all over Trent in the quad. Flirting with him in front of me and then I find out she's been sending him pics.

Nick Trent's phone from his bag and it doesn't take long to find them. Pics she's sent to him that make me gag, her in underwear, looks like a whore, her in a swimming pool, then her nude in her bedroom, heaps of cheap stuffed toys on the pink bed in the background.

Trent looks all red and mad says / *My fucking phone's been nicked.*

TRENT: My fucking phone's been nicked.

SAM: I say it straight up. I nicked it Trent. Knew something was going on and look what I find. I hold up the pic of the fat cow's tits and his mouth opens so wide I could punch out all his crooked teeth.

Who is she?

TRENT: No-one.

SAM: No-one? Then what the fuck are all these pics? What's her name dickhead don't just dribble. Speak up you arsehole and tell me her name.

TRENT: Chante.

Eryn Jean Norvill and Elena Carapetis in the 2012 Q Theatre production at the Seymour Centre. (Photo © Amanda James)

SAM: Chante? What an ugly name.

Well you two can be together. It's over.

So over.

Break up video in my head like Rihanna post Chris Brown.

Yeah. I look sad but… I'm planning revenge.

Chante. Chante. Two and two together.

That was then and now…

When I overheard her name on the phone I realised who Chante is. And who spawned her.

I change my plan with the counsellor now. I'm going to talk and talk and then… when the time is ripe… I'll ambush her.

Sitting there after school in the demountable now. Flies circling above us and her with her sweat marks and I see Chante looks just like her mum. Fat cow with a pig nose. Her tired eyes looking at me as she's saying.

MICHELLE: I'm glad you're talking now Sam. It makes it easier when you open up.

SAM: I feel like laughing out loud and challenging that, let's just see how easy it gets. I ask her *what I am meant to call you*, she smiles says,

MICHELLE: Call me Michelle.

SAM: I tell Michelle what she wants to hear about my home life. I say that Mum read in some Christian magazine that the way to ensure your daughter doesn't go off the rails is to sit down every day and talk about things so we talk every night before dinner. When Dad and my brother are out and it's just us. Sometimes we cut up carrots or beans and we talk. Sometimes we have a glass of wine but I have to scull if Dad comes through the door. Dad's princess doesn't drink.

Mum thinks our conversations are deep but I just tell her what she wants to hear.

MICHELLE: And what is that?

SAM *shrugs.*

I'm sure your mum would like to know the truth.

SAM: I thought that too until after you know what happened. Do you know what their solution to it all was? Send me to you and to a Catholic school. Send me a school run by a barren old nuns and never speak about it again.

MICHELLE: Maybe they don't know what to say.

SAM *laughs.*

SAM: I ask Michelle about all the stuff on the internet.

MICHELLE: What do you mean?

SAM: Like what happens to it all? Like say a kid gets run over by a truck or shot in the head by some drugged up emo loser freak in some school in America what happens to their facebook page? Who answers their email messages? Who turns the whole thing off or does it just keep living? Does the inbox just keeping getting spam?

She never knows what to say.

MICHELLE: Maybe the parents…

SAM: Nobody's parents have their passwords Michelle.

I want to tell her maybe I'm worried about all the pics of me that Trent has. How they might live on like some dead kid's facebook.

She's happy to let me talk. Weird she never just asks me. *Why did you do it?*

I let her make me tea. I eat all her biscuits. She even starts bringing in Tim Tams for me.

And I have a silver gun like a film star and I am loading it up with bullets.

I take two Tim Tams. Says:

It makes me sad thinking about how girls lose their virginity.

MICHELLE: What do you mean by that Sam?

SAM: I mean it sucks. One guy was an arsehole. And I reel her right in and line her up for target practice.

I start to cry and I say

He knew it was my first time but he wasn't romantic, he didn't care.

He took pictures of me naked, made me send him pictures of myself and showed his mates. He put them up online and when I asked him to take them down he laughed at me.

He didn't want to use condoms and after a while he made me promise I'd go on the pill. Then I found out he was fucking other girls as well.

I found pics of other girls on his phone.

I broke it off with him and I was lucky.

Finger on the trigger.

'Cause I never used his name up until then and so I aim and I say

I found pictures of another girl on Trent's phone.

Chante. This girl Chante.

Fire. Bang. Bang.

Poor Chante everyone blogging that she's a slut. Pretty sad pictures. Looked like she was in her mum's knickers and then there were pics of her nude. Poor thing. He's shown all his mates and put them online he's gonna be a pedo when he gets older he's so sick.

Bullets fired and I'm waiting for blood.

MICHELLE: You enjoying this Sam?

SAM: What do you mean?

MICHELLE: I mean are you enjoying putting me through this? I don't even want to know if it's true but even if it is it doesn't matter because this isn't about Chante or me or our lives… this is about you. You want to intimidate me? Make me feel scared like some girl at your school?

SAM: No.

MICHELLE: I'm not scared of you. Why would I be scared?

Take a look at yourself Sam. At what you do. What you did. Not about the way it might have looked in a movie or a video clip but about the reality of what you did. To your best friend. To yourself.

I have been trying to figure out something about you. Where do you live? Not the house or the street or the suburb but in here. If you can't see the difference between what's going on in there and what's happening around you, what'll happen to you?

SAM: Michelle's spat on her blouse and knocked a Tim Tam on the floor.

No idea what you're on about. Gotta go.

We hear swarming and trucks passing at high speed.

KELLY/AISHA: Then

KELLY: New guy at the food court.

AISHA: Noah's cousin. / Torquan.

KELLY: Torquan.

KELLY: He doesn't go to school, works on the roads. Torquan knows he's good looking. He's seen the school girls watch him, he's felt the eyes of every lady from Shoe-Deeni to GOLO look him up and down. He leans back on a chair in the food court looking bored. Noah brings him donuts.

AISHA: I stand between Gloria Jean's and Chinky Chonk's waiting for Sam, watch them, him and Noah. The way Noah's looking at his cousin.

KELLY: Then Torquan sees Aish filming them. He sits up, his mouth snarls and he points at her. / They're coming over.

AISHA: They're coming over. Torquan first then, another one of their gang followed by Noah. Torquan says /

TORQUAN: Why were you filming us?

AISHA: His breath is stale cigarettes his green eyes are cold.

TORQUAN: Why were you filming us?

AISHA: He grabs the phone out of my hand and plays back the film.

TORQUAN: Oh look at that Noah, she's got you on film. Why you filming my cousin, freak?

AISHA: Noah looks down at his feet.

KELLY: Torquan grabs Noah's donuts, takes one out and squashes it on the phone.

AISHA: Takes another one out and squashes it in my hair. His mates are laughing and a table load of boys behind him start cheering then Noah tells him to stop and Sam comes up behind us. She gets in between Torquan and me and says:

SAM: What the fuck are you animals doing to my friend?

TORQUAN: *Teaching her a lesson.*

SAM: Teaching her a lesson?

TORQUAN: *Yeah.*

AISHA: My phone ringing now. Mum Mum Mum flashing on the screen. Torquan grabs the phone, answers it says: /

TORQUAN: *Hello Mum she can't come right now 'cause she's sucking my dick.*

AISHA: I close my eyes and start to cry.

Sam yelling to get the phone back. Torquan saying it's his phone now. Footsteps, security comes, some guy says sort things out or you can leave and then I hear something smashing. I open my eyes and Torquan is smashing my phone hard against this giant plastic kebab. The phone scatters in pieces on the food court floor.

I'm led outside. Sam and Kelly both pat me like I'm a dog. Kelly strokes my hair while Sam tries to put my phone back together. She gives up, chucks it the ashtrays near the entrance to the food court.

I'm shivering.

SAM: Torquan's such an arsehole.

SAM/KELLY: What were you filming them for?

SAM: Shouldn't have filmed them. I don't get you.

AISHA: I look at them and can't explain.

An awkward pause, then SAM *reveals a magazine.*

SAM: Look what I nicked.

KELLY: *Cosmo*.

SAM: Sealed section's back.

KELLY: Open it. Open it.

AISHA: They peel it back like hungry dogs.

SAM: The great *Cosmo* boobs and bottoms match up game. Look at him!

AISHA: Photos of naked white guys with vegetables over their bits.

SAM: And him.

AISHA: Their fronts and their behinds.

KELLY: Hot arse. Look at his tats.

AISHA: Next page, girls with roses or orchids covering their vulvas… all of them smiling for the camera. All of them white.

KELLY: Look Aisha.

AISHA: Yeah I can see.

SAM: She's upset about her phone.

KELLY: I got a spare one, you can borrow that.

KELLY: What's wrong Aish?

Tell us Aish? You're a skank you can say whatever you want.

AISHA: A skank?

SAM: Yeah.

AISHA: Do you know what that means? What that says about us? Mum keeps asking what that means. I can't tell my friends at home that now I'm here I'm a skank.

SAM: It's like, a joke.

AISHA: Nobody else I know gets it.

SAM: So?

AISHA: Don't you see?

SAM: No.

AISHA: I just didn't think things would be so hard here. I don't understand anything. I thought things were going so well. When I started school and I met you two and when we went to that party I met that guy and I thought… I felt really close to you both but…

KELLY: What?

AISHA: Is this what being a skank is?

SAM *has rolled up the magazine and she's hitting her hand with it.* KELLY *looks away.*

I don't want to have to spend my life lying.

Lying about where I am going. Lying about where I have been. Lying about who I am with.

Why is everything here a series of lies or dares or…

Kelly you never tell us what you feel about your dad. Sam you always seem so mad about everything and I don't understand why. This place is so cold. The way you all treat each other. And I'm just a curry and I feel so left out.

SAM: Then go back.

KELLY: Sam!

SAM: No. If you don't like the way we do things here why did you come?

AISHA: I didn't /

SAM: You don't want to be a skank then don't be.

I just stuck up for you. I just saved you from those black cunts and what? All you can say is you don't like it here?

Why don't you take your stinky family and go back?

AISHA: I wasn't saying that I /

SAM: You stuck up bitch. How dare you judge us when the place you come from must suck or you wouldn't have left. I don't want you hanging around us anymore. We don't want you.

Take your fucking ugly curry eating family and get back on the fucking boat. Nobody asked you to come here. You don't like the way we live here? Then fuck off back home.

AISHA: I didn't mean /

SAM: Don't talk to me again bitch.

SAM *whacks* AISHA *with the rolled up magazine and leaves.*

Come on Kelly.

KELLY *hesitates then finally follows* SAM. AISHA *is left alone. After a time she gets up and leaves. A projection: ants running about.*

KELLY: Now.

> The waiting room.
> Same smell, same posters, same nurses, same doctor. Josie again.

JOSIE: Hello Kelly.

KELLY: Same room, same chair.

> She holds an envelope. Inside it the results of the tests.
>
> For HIV.
>
> > KELLY *stares at the envelope.*

JOSIE: How are you doing?

KELLY: Been alright but I don't want to talk, want to rip that envelope open so I know, so I…?

JOSIE: I've already looked at your results.

KELLY: Heart pumping in my ears. And?

JOSIE: They're fine. All negative.

KELLY: You're sure? It's not a mistake or something is it?

> / I'm fine?

JOSIE: You're fine.

KELLY: Do I have to come back again in three months or anything?

JOSIE: No. That's it.

KELLY: So I can just go?

JOSIE: You can go. But…

KELLY: Yeah?

JOSIE: I have been thinking about you a lot. I have been wondering something and… I think I just need to ask you this straight up.

KELLY: Yeah?

JOSIE: What made you do it?

SAM: How it started?

KELLY: You mean how what we did started?

SAM/KELLY: It was her idea.

KELLY: She said that but /

SAM: It was our idea.

> It's lunch at school. I'm sick to death of standing in the sun. Sick to death of how the guys get all the good places to hang out and how we are stuck there like fucking cows in a field so I say let's get out of here. Just the two of us.

KELLY: Out the school gates and up the highway, really hot day but it feels good being out of school. Nobody staring.

SAM: And we've gotten away from Aisha.

KELLY: Still feel shit about that.

SAM: Bullshit.

KELLY: I do. What we did. How we froze her out.

SAM: She deserves it. She's a real pain in the arse Kelly.

SAM/KELLY: Just the two of us.

SAM: Like it should be.

KELLY: Out of school.

SAM: Walking up the highway.

KELLY: No balls flying past /

SAM: No boys shouting shit at us /

KELLY: Just cars and trucks speeding past.

SAM: A hot shirtless guy in a red car passes beeps his horn and / we wave at him.

KELLY: We wave at him.

SAM: Some hot guy in a red car.

KELLY: How it feels when he does that, and it doesn't matter if he beeped at you or at me, how I feel is like we are on some adventure while everybody else is stuck in the real world in that fucking hot horrible playground, there we are… like in some video clip.

Sam and Kelly sing the first three verses of 'Your Love Is My Drug' by Ke$ha.

SAM: We could be running away you know. Escaping forever.

KELLY: You changing out of your school clothes? We're going back aren't we? After lunch.

SAM: Maybe.

KELLY: Traffic passes on the road.

SAM: One truck after the other.

KELLY: None slow down.

SAM: None turn in.

KELLY: None notice us, walking like ants in the sun.

They both raise their arms up and scream.

SAM: We are alive. We not sitting in some fucking classroom reading about the world.

KELLY: No /

SAM: We are living /

KELLY: Bell for class rings in the distance. / We keep walking.

SAM: We keep walking.

Sign up ahead.

KELLY: 'Rest Area'.

SAM: You look at me and grin the same grin you had on your face when we tried speed I remember what you said that night when the speed came on you said / It's like I'm at the top of a roller coaster.

KELLY: It's like I'm at the top of a roller coaster.

Where we going Sam?

SAM: Just up here. Peace and quiet. / Then we are at the truck stop.

KELLY: Then we are at the truck stop.

SAM: Just the sound of the highway. / Nobody here.

KELLY: Nobody here. Just us in the dust. Flies on your back.

SAM: Brush 'em off then.

Magpie on a picnic table.

Go on scare it off hate magpies fuck off.

KELLY: Scare it off, sit reading the shit people scribble on tables. Jonny for Nerrida.

SAM: Johnny roots Kylie.

KELLY: John eats out Cathy's cunt.

SAM: I'm sixteen with a big fat cock wanna suck?

KELLY: Where's the action? Been looking all day? Want some action call me.

SAM: Want a smoke?

They smoke.

Give us your phone. Let's ring the guy with the big fat cock.

KELLY: What for?

SAM: What do you reckon?

They laugh.

What would you do if your dad drove in and stopped?

Pause.

Eryn Jean Norvill as Sam in the 2012 Q Theatre production at the Seymour Centre. (Photo © Amanda James)

KELLY: We talk about sex.

You tell me about how out of control things got with Trent. The look on his face when you finally dumped him. How you wish you hadn't lost your virginity to him 'cause he came so quick.

SAM: And when I ask you about virginity you tell me that you lost your ages ago and I laugh at you and say bullshit!

Pause.

Do you want to talk about it?

KELLY: No truck driver pulls up that day.

AISHA: Go to Westfield after school, food court smell of meat. I sit alone near Donut King wait for something, anything to happen. Nothing does.

Go home. Sit online alone.

I'm on Facebook checking to see if Kelly dumped me yet and there's a friend request. From Noah. From Noah Futemana. Message says I'm really sorry Aisha. Hope I can make it up to you.

KELLY/SAM: Next day at lunch, we go back.

SAM: Did you see Aisha this morning?

KELLY: Yeah.

SAM: Think she's finally got the message?

KELLY: Yeah. Looked straight through her.

SAM: Me too. Froze that bitch off like a wart.

They laugh.

We go to the truck stop every day now.

KELLY: We sit there at lunch.

SAM: Don't do the mall no more.

KELLY: We change out of our uniforms in case someone dobs us in and /

SAM: Sit on that picnic table / at the Truck Stop.

KELLY: At the Truck Stop.

KELLY: Quieter than anywhere else.

SAM: Our picnic table.

SAM/KELLY: Just us.

Pause.

SAM: The day it first happens.

KELLY: We get there and there is a truck parked right up the end.

A truck with a bowl of fruit on the side.

SAM: Anyone in it?

KELLY: Can't see.

SAM: Just sit at the table.

KELLY: You got a smoke?

They smoke.

SAM: We talk and shit. Look at the cover of a magazine I nicked.

KELLY: *Boys boys men* written on the cover.

SAM: And *sex moves that'll rattle his brain for days.*

KELLY: Article promises to tell the way to find your perfect sex match.
You reading it out / when

SAM: When this guy gets out of the truck. Shit. Look.

KELLY: You see him first. I'm reading and you stop me.

They watch him in silence.

SAM: This young dude /

KELLY: Tanned with thick legs /

SAM: Tanned with tattoos / This dude who drives the fruit truck is / HOT!

KELLY: HOT. He doesn't see us.

SAM: He walks around the truck looking at the tyres.

KELLY: Bends over. Look at that.

SAM: What's he looking at you reckon?

KELLY: Dunno.

SAM: You reckon he's seen us?

KELLY: No. Do you?

SAM: Dunno. No.

They watch him.

KELLY: The magazine pages flutter in the wind.

SAM *lights a smoke.*

SAM: This is like some video clip.

KELLY: I lean back, camera on me.

SAM: Stand up play with my hair, camera on me.

KELLY: Then he turns around. Camera on us. / He sees us.

SAM: He sees us.

KELLY: Don't know whether to wave. Or /

SAM: Don't look at him. Read the magazine.

KELLY: He forgets his tyres, looks this way for ages.

He's looking at us.

SAM: Shut up.

KELLY: He can't hear me.

They giggle.

What should we do?

SAM: Camera on him. He leans against the truck, lights a cigarette.

Go over to him. Say hello.

KELLY: Me? Why don't you?

SAM: I will if you want but… I dare you to. Double dare /

KELLY: What'll I say?

SAM: Ask him where he's going?

KELLY: Then what?

SAM: Ask him if he's tired.

KELLY: Then what?

SAM: For fuck's sake Kelly. I don't know. If you like him… ask him if you can make his journey better.

KELLY: Make his journey better? You mean…

SAM: Fuck it. Do you want me to do it?

KELLY: No. I'll go.

SAM: Then go.

KELLY: I will. Mind my bag.

> KELLY *walks towards him.*

Gravel and dirt under my feet sweat under my arms. What am I doing? He's looking at me now. I want to look back, check if Sam's watching but I can't. I just keep going.

SAM: Sun beats down, flies everywhere and Kelly stands in front of the truck driver.

KELLY: I am close to him now. Smell his sweat his cigarette. I stop in front of him. Look up and see my face reflected in his sunglasses. Say it /

SAM: Say it.

Where are you going?

Are you tired?

Don't just stand there.

SAM/KELLY: Is there something I can do to make your journey /

> KELLY *reaches down and lifts up her t-shirt.*

> *We hear flies seething.*

AISHA: Facebook chat: Noah.

NOAH: *Have to walk my dog after school want to meet me in the park?*

AISHA: Don't like dogs don't want to say no. I go.

He's sitting at a picnic table with a bag of donuts. The dog's asleep at his feet, says

NOAH: She's old she can't hear.

AISHA: He looks at me for ages, says /

NOAH: Sorry.

AISHA: Looks at his feet, says /

NOAH: I really like you.

AISHA: Looks at his hands, says /

NOAH: Maybe we could… go out.

AISHA: You mean?

NOAH: Yeah.

AISHA: Okay.

Noah and me. We're going out.

SAM: Kelly's in the truck. I sit at the picnic table waiting.

Flies seethe everywhere, questions seethe in my head. I think of backpacker killers and rapists on TV, thinking too much and the seething sounds all around me, listen to my iPod.

A brown car drives in some woman with a dog.

Dog runs towards me, I pat it and then it shits near my bag.

Your dog's done a shit.

Want to leave.

Fifty flies squat on my bag. Highway buzzes. Wish you weren't in the truck. Wish you'd come back.

Long pause. Flies and highway noise.

The truck door opens.

The truck door shuts.

Truck engine starts. Rumbles away.

KELLY *walks towards* SAM. *She looks calm. She reaches into her pocket and pulls a $50 note, holds it up, it waves in the breeze.*

Shit!

KELLY: I know.

SAM: I can't believe you did that. That you…

What happened?

How was it?

KELLY: Guess you'll have to find out for yourself. / Why we did it?

SAM: Why we did it? I didn't think about that much.

KELLY: I wondered that when I was sitting alone at the picnic table. When Sam went and I was waiting with the bags and the phone.

SAM: That was the deal.

KELLY: One of us went and one stayed to keep watch, ready with the phone to ring fuck knows who or say fuck knows what.

SAM: Didn't think about what people would say if they found out.

KELLY: When we weren't there life went on as normal.

SAM: Nobody I know talks about truck drivers.

SAM/KELLY: Why we did it?

KELLY: Money?

SAM: It gave me a rush.

KELLY: It was pretty easy money.

SAM: When we were sitting there waiting and a truck came in it was like…

KELLY: Speed and a shot of tequila with your favourite song full blast.

SAM: Being a long long way from everything you knew.

KELLY: Trucks with all sorts of shit in them and we keep a record, a list in the back of a book.

KELLY: Blueberries /

SAM: Lambs /

KELLY: Milk /

SAM: Beer /

KELLY: Sand /

SAM: Shampoo /

KELLY: Petrol, baked beans.

SAM: Hamburger patties, calves.

There was this fat bloke. He'd just eaten McDonald's. Stunk of special sauce and there was a French-fry in the crease of his shorts when he unzipped it. I wanted to…

KELLY: Second guy wasn't like the first /

SAM: Turn back. Wanted to…

KELLY: Second guy was old. I wanted to take it back when I said / can I make your journey better?

SAM: Can I make your journey better?

KELLY: I wanted to turn around and run back to the picnic table but then he offered me a Starburst, a smoke, changed the radio station and

Rihanna came on and / I just closed my eyes.

SAM: I just closed my eyes. Got it done.

KELLY: I hoped the first guy'd come back. Dude with the fruit. 'Cause most of the others were /

SAM: Old with hairy ears and shit.

KELLY: Never really talked about it much. Made a joke about it but never really spoke about what we were doing. And I want to ask you Sam, how far do you go?

And I wanted to ask you Sam, when you're in there, in the truck, how do you feel? But…

SAM: After the first week we have cash. / Cashed-up bitches!

KELLY: Cashed-up bitches! Go into the city /

SAM: Shop in the city.

KELLY: We sit on the train next to each other and I want to ask… but I don't say a word. I want to say something, anything but don't know how to start.

Something between us, something different.

SAM: It didn't go for that long.

KELLY: Wasn't long at all.

SAM/KELLY: The feeling, when I hear sound of the trucks pulling in.

SAM: It makes me feel thrilled, that never fades /

KELLY: It begins to fill me with dread.

SAM: Just before it ends we're sitting there.

KELLY: I hear a / truck.

SAM: Truck on the gravel, pulls in stops, and the driver, / this big fat dude gets out of his truck.

KELLY: This big fat dude gets out of his truck. Walks towards us smiling. Tells us some guy on the CB had told him to check us out.

SAM: Some guy on the radio told him…

KELLY: The CB / radio

SAM: Radio… We're stars… People who don't even know us talking about us. We're famous. Famous. / Famous! Then things change.

KELLY: Famous. Then things change.

SAM: That day /

KELLY: This driver.

I go up to his truck.

Look up to the mirror.

Knock on the door climb up look through and he's eating a ham sandwich listening to the radio.

Winds down his window and I'm holding onto the side of the truck leaning back smiling saying…

SAM: He rings the cops.

KELLY: He just stares at me. The look on his face when I say what I say. Crucifix swinging from his mirror.

SAM: Fucking Christians.

KELLY: Takes a while but the cops figure it out.

SAM: And that Friday.

KELLY: After school.

SAM: We're just sitting there at the picnic table and / then a cop car pulls up.

KELLY: Then a cop car pulls up and / we turn and run.

SAM: We turn and run. Like fugitives in a movie.

KELLY: Just like a movie.

SAM: They chase us /

KELLY: We scream /

SAM: Footsteps, dust.

KELLY: A big hand on my shoulder.

SAM: The cop that catches me is kinda hot.

KELLY: Cops take us back to school.

SAM: Make us wait outside the office.

KELLY: I'm shitting myself.

SAM: We weren't doing anything.

KELLY: Hushed voices and shit inside. And us out there.

SAM: We weren't doing nothing.

KELLY: How much do they know? What do you reckon they're telling her?

How much do you reckon they know?

Sam? Sam? How much do you /

SAM: Shut the fuck up. For fuck's sake shut up for once Kelly. Shut up and don't say a word. If you do. /

KELLY: What?

SAM: I'll fucking kill you.

KELLY: Rowse opens the door.

SAM: Her and the cop glare at me like I killed someone.

KELLY: They call you in. Leave me alone with dead flowers in a vase, the cleaner down the end of the hall fiddles with a vacuum chord.

SAM: Cop stares at me.

Rowse stares at me.

KELLY: / Real quiet.

SAM: Real quiet, Rowse asks:

ROWSE: What were you two doing out there?

SAM: And again:

ROWSE: What were you doing out there?

SAM: Then one more fucking time.

ROWSE/SAM/KELLY: What were you two doing out there?

KELLY: I hear her shout and then nothing.

SAM: Cop wants to look inside my bag.

ROWSE: Your parents have been notified.

SAM *shrugs.*

SAM: I keep tight hold of my bag and I say nothing.

ROWSE: Samantha, what were you doing out there?

SAM: Say nothing. Just stare straight back at them like a bad arse bitch in a cop show. Clock ticks. / Tick tock on the clock and the party won't…

KELLY: Tick tock on the clock and the party won't…

SAM: That's all they hear, I don't say zip.

Then they send me out. / They call her in.

KELLY: They call me in.

SAM/KELLY: We swap chairs.

KELLY: I'm in the hot seat.

SAM: I'm out in the hallway.

KELLY: The cop sighs. He looks at me and then he says that the truck driver didn't mean any trouble. Has a daughter about our age. Just wanted to protect us.

Rowse and the cop stare and I know I'm meant to say nothing, keep my mouth shut, I know I'm meant to but…

SAM: Dare.
KELLY: No.
SAM: Double dare.
KELLY: No.
SAM: Double dog dick dare.
KELLY: No. Truth.

>   KELLY *begins to cry.*

SAM: I hear Kelly crying, hear that stupid bitch sobbing like she's on
Judge Judy.

I know she's gonna tell them everything.

So I stand up. I open the door and they all look at me.

ROWSE: Samantha how dare you barge in here.
SAM: But I say it.

It was her idea. She thought it up. She did it first.

She was gagging for it. She wanted it so bad and she couldn't get it
anywhere else.

She was fucking them weren't you Kelly?

She was fucking them and I wasn't. I'm not a slut like her.

>   SAM *and* KELLY *stare at each other.*

>   *The slapping sound.*

AISHA: In the middle of the quad.

Slap like a whip. Everyone hears it. Stops.

Kelly snatches Sam's hair twists it round her wrist. Sam's down on
the ground. Kelly shouting Sam screams, kids in a circle around
them, phones held overhead.

Teachers rip them apart.

Noah's next to me in the quad. He reaches out, squeezes my hand.
We walk away.

>   AISHA *leaves.*

>   *We see* KELLY *sitting and staring into nothingness, the blue light
>   of a television. She watches without distraction.*

SAM: Now. Right now. And it's my birthday tomorrow. Turning fifteen. Mum gave me my present early, tickets to the Ke$ha concert. Most embarrassing night of my life. Mum took me but she looked so out of place. She bought all this glitter and shit so she could cover up her wrinkles, she said it was so *we could bond again.*

There were all these hot guys there and they could tell she was a freak all I did was try to lose her. Didn't enjoy the music at all.

My new school sucks but it's better than being at that shithole by the highway. Not that many friends yet. On the weekend I was so bored I even cleaned up my room. Chucked out stuff, tiaras and princess shit Dad bought for me.

I'm not a princess, I'm not a movie star. I'm a…

Bitch. I'm a bitch. I've been a total bitch to everyone.

I thought my life was a music clip or a movie. But it is not. I guess I'm just…

The fly circles around the room. Around me.

Camera pans in.

Close up on my eyes, on the tear as it dribbles over my cheekbones.

On my lips. Music starts.

Camera circles round me.

> SAM *watches* KELLY *watch television. She almost makes her way to speak to her but instead turns and leaves.* KELLY *is alone. The television blares on.*

> *We hear some bland talk show which in turn blurs into 'Love Song Dedications'.*

MERCER: 'Love Song Dedications'. You're with Richard Mercer on the coldest night of the year. Just the kind of night to snuggle by the fire… I've got Kelly on the line. Thinking of someone special on this chilly night?

KELLY: Yes.

MERCER: What is his name?

KELLY: Dad.

MERCER: Dad. And if Dad is out here listening Kelly, what would you like to say to him?

KELLY: I missed him but now it's okay.

MERCER: It's okay Kelly?

KELLY: Yes. He said he could protect me. He said while he was around nothing bad would ever happen to me again. But he left. And if he's out there listening I want to say to him that it wouldn't have mattered anyway.

Mum acts like you're dead and I'm not going to stick around here. Maybe I'll see you one day. But just… need you to know. I don't need protecting anymore.

Day fades to night. KELLY *continues to watch television. Insects call, becoming louder and louder.*

Then silence.

THE END

www.ingramcontent.com/pod-product-compliance
Lightning Source LLC
Chambersburg PA
CBHW050022090426
42734CB00021B/3383